Rice Is Nice

Nancy Noel Williams

 TeachingStrategies® · Bethesda, MD

For Teaching Strategies, LLC.
Publisher: Larry Bram
Editorial Director: Hilary Parrish Nelson
VP Curriculum and Assessment: Cate Heroman
Product Manager: Kai-leé Berke
Book Development Team: Sherrie Rudick and Jan Greenberg
Project Manager: Jo A. Wilson

For Q2AMedia
Editorial Director: Bonnie Dobkin
Editor and Curriculum Adviser: Suzanne Barchers
Program Manager: Gayatri Singh
Creative Director: Simmi Sikka
Project Manager: Santosh Vasudevan
Designers: Ritu Chopra & Shruti Aggarwal
Picture Researchers: Judy Brown & Stephanie Mills

Picture Credits
t-top b-bottom c-center l-left r-right

Cover: Masterfile.

Back Cover: Photostogo: tl, Dusan Zidar/Fotolia: tr, Photostogo: bl, Rohit Seth/Dreamstime: br.

Title page: Malinhk/Dreamstime.

Insides: Photostogo: 3, Alena Yakusheva/Dreamstime: 4t, Radius Images/Jupiter Images: 4b, Imgorthand/Istockphoto: 5tl, Q2AMedia Image Bank:5tr, Carrie Bottomley/Istockphoto: 5b, Robert Churchill/istockphoto: 6, Dejan Suc/Istockphoto: 7, Brand X Pictures/Photolibrary: 8, Photostogo: 9tr, Photostogo: 9tl, Rohit Seth/ Dreamstime: 9b, Q2AMedia Image Bank: 10, Malinhk/Dreamstime: 11, Kati Molin/Dreamstime: 12l, Marc Dietrich/Dreamstime: 12r, Q2AMedia Image Bank: 12c, Rmarmion/Dreamstime: 13, Anna Chelnokova/Dreamstime: 14, Torsten Ståhlberg/Istockphoto: 15, Istockphoto: 16t, Cedric Carter/Istockphoto: 16bl, Ferenc Ungor/123RF: 16br, Q2AMedia Image Bank: 17, Q2AMedia Image Bank: 18, Q2AMedia Image Bank: 19, Dusan Zidar/Fotolia: 20, Monkey Business Images/Dreamstime: 21, Scott Rothstein/Dreamstime: 22tl, Renata Osinska/Dreamstime: 22tr, Photostogo: 22b, Monkey Business Images: 23, Photostogo: 24tl, Photostogo: 24tm, Dusan Zidar/Fotolia: 24tr, Photostogo: 24ml, Boris Katsman/Istockphoto: 24m, David G. Freund/Istockphoto: 24mr, Photostogo: 24bl, Istockphoto: 24bm, Rohit Seth/Dreamstime: 24br.

Teaching Strategies, LLC.
Bethesda, MD
www.TeachingStrategies.com

ISBN: 978-1-60617-144-8

Library of Congress Cataloging-in-Publication Data
Williams, Nancy Noel.
  Rice is nice / Nancy Noel Williams.
    p. cm.
  ISBN 978-1-60617-144-8
  1. Rice--Juvenile literature. 2. Cookery (Rice)--Juvenile literature. I. Title.
  SB191.R5W483 2010
  641.3'318--dc22

                          2009037268

CPSIA tracking label information:
RR Donnelley, Shenzhen, China
Date of Production: March 2018
Cohort: Batch 6

Printed and bound in China

8 9 10 11	18
Printing	Year Printed

People all over the world love to eat rice!
Why? Because rice is good to eat.
It gives people energy!

Rice is the most important food for more than half the people in the world. Many babies, children, and grown-ups eat rice every day.

Some people eat rice with chopsticks. Others eat rice with a fork or a spoon.

5

Rice is grown in two different ways.
Lowland rice is grown in flooded fields.
The water comes from rain or rivers.

Some rice farmers depend on rainfall to grow upland rice. They may grow rice in terraces like these.

Rice grains come in three sizes.

Medium grain rice

Long grain rice

Short grain rice

Short grain rice
is often sticky.

Medium grain rice
is often fluffy. So
is long grain rice.

Rice comes in different colors, too.
Do you like brown rice or white rice?

Rice can even be red or black!

Black rice

White rice

Red rice

Many foods are made from rice.

Rice milk and rice tea are good to drink.

Rice noodles are made from rice flour.

Rice cakes are good with jam on top!

Did you know that rice can also be used to make things we do not eat?

Rice paper was used to make these colorful umbrellas.

Paper made from rice straw is used
in art or for beautiful lanterns.

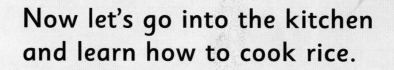

Now let's go into the kitchen
and learn how to cook rice.

Begin by washing your rice.

Combine the rice with water. It's as simple as 1-2-3! 1 cup of raw rice + 2 cups of water = 3 cups of cooked rice.

Put the rice and water in a pot. Boil the rice on the stove. Or, you can use a special rice cooker.

Turn down the heat and cover the pot. When the rice has soaked up the water, it is ready to eat.

You can add toppings and sauce! Your rice can be sweet and sour, tangy, or spicy.

You can have rice for breakfast, lunch, or dinner. It's always delicious!

Have you had your rice today?

Rice Dishes
Around the World

Fried Rice
China

Biryani
India

Chicken Risotto
Italy

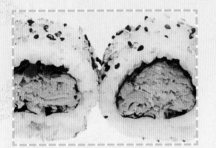

Sushi
Japan

Meat Plov
Russia

Pilaf
Lebanon

Paella
Spain

Jok with Fish Ball
Thailand

Red Beans and Rice
United States